the
drawings
of
Michelangelo

Introduction by

BY **IRVING STONE**

Author of "The Agony and the Ecstasy"
A biographical novel of Michelangelo

BORDEN PUBLISHING COMPANY

LOS ANGELES

MICHELANGELO BUONARROTI

1475-1565

MICHELANGELO BUONARROTI was born in 1475 in Caprese; his father was serving there as visiting mayor, visiting, that is, from Florence, where the Buonarroti family boasted of having paid taxes for over three hundred years. He was Florentine and Tuscan to his marrow.

Michelangelo began to draw as naturally as he began to breathe. According to Tolnay, he drew a Triton on a wall of the Buonarroti villa in Settignano while still a boy. He did poorly in Greek and Latin at Urbino's grammar school because he preferred to draw in the margins of his notebook, or play hooky in the Brancacci Chapel of Santa Maria del Carmine to copy the Masaccios.

At thirteen, three years too late according to Tuscan tradition, he was apprenticed to Ghirlandaio, though he wanted to become a sculptor rather than a painter. "It is not my trade," he would tell Pope Julius II when the Holy Father ordered him to paint the Sistine Chapel. But the last of the long line of Florentine sculpture studios had vanished; and Michelangelo was determined to become *some kind of artist.*

From this moment until his death, only a few months short of ninety, Michelangelo never ceased to draw.

Bernard Berenson says in his *Drawings of the Florentine Painters:* "The pen work in these early drawings, and indeed more than one trick of shorthand of later date, tell truthfully that Ghirlandaio was the man who first put a pen into Michelangelo's hand and taught him how to use it."

Michelangelo knew that drawing was the best way to achieve authority of eye and hand. He never moved forward to marble or paint until he had put a solid ground of draughtsmanship beneath him. Hundreds upon hundreds of drawings went into his exploration of the line, form, structure, tension, the meaning of every phase of a sculpture or fresco. The David is not one piece of sculpture, any more than is the Moses, Pieta, Bruges Madonna or Dawn and Dusk; for each arm, neck, back, knee, elbow, hand, head, endless experimental drawings were tried.

What was Michelangelo seeking through these thousands of drawings, most of which he burned when he had completed a project? Truth. If I may be permitted to plagiarize myself, drawing was for Michelangelo the supreme way of blotting out his ignorance of a subject, and establishing wisdom in its place. Drawing was a candle to be lighted so that the sculptor did not have to grope in the dark; a plan for understanding the structure at which he was gazing.

For Michelangelo drawing was learning, a measuring stick to see how much honesty there was in him. It revealed Michelangelo to himself. All his life he worshipped Dante, and for him drawing was akin to the poet's written line, set down to see if there was a truth worth revealing. His only sculpture maestro, Bertoldo, who trained him in Lorenzo de' Medici's sculpture garden, said:

"To draw is to be like God when he put life into Adam; it is the outer breathing of the artist and the inner breathing of the model that creates a new third life on paper. Drawing is an act of love."

Michelangelo is conceded to be the world's greatest sculptor; by many art historians he is thought to be the greatest of all painters. Drawing, for the eighty years of his life as an artist, was his starting point, his *modus operandi,* the mechanism by means of which he sought, and ultimately found, his own rare combination of beauty and truth. He could no more have created his masterpieces in marble and paint without drawing than he could have without his hands.

The High Renaissance, which Michelangelo brought to its culminating peak, is based solidly on the indispensible craft of draughtsmanship.

IRVING STONE

Cover Drawing
Profile with Fantastic Head-Dress
ASHMOLEAN MUSEUM, OXFORD, ENGLAND

Head of Lazarus

Black chalk over red chalk

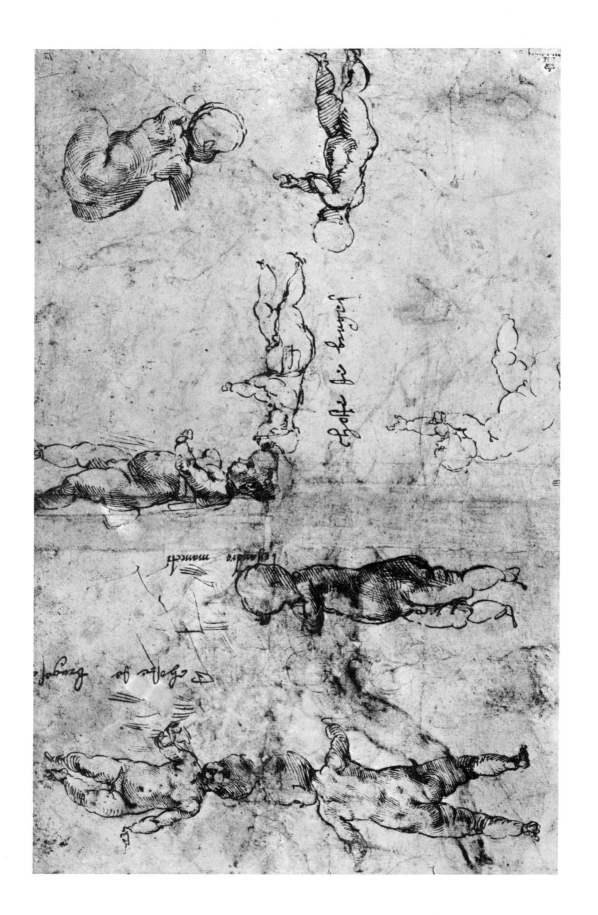

Eight Nude Children

Pen and ink

THE BRITISH MUSEUM, LONDON, ENGLAND

Study for the Left Arm of the "Night" in the Medici Chapel
Black chalk and pen and ink
THE BRITISH MUSEUM, LONDON, ENGLAND

Study of a Youth with Arm in the Pose of Apollo Belvedere

Pen and Ink

THE BRITISH MUSEUM, LONDON, ENGLAND

Venus, Mars and Cupid

Black chalk

UFFIZI GALLERY, FLORENCE, ITALY

Profile with Fantastic Head-Dress

Red chalk

ASHMOLEAN MUSEUM, OXFORD, ENGLAND

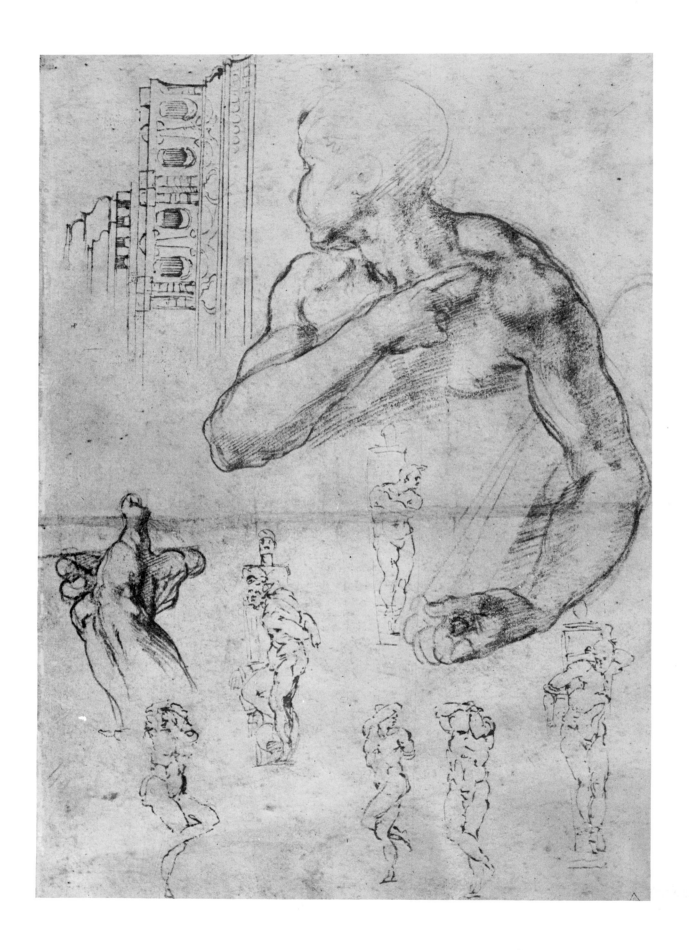

Sketches for the Sistine Frecoes and for the Tomb of Julius

Red chalk and pen and ink

ASHMOLEAN MUSEUM, OXFORD, ENGLAND

Sketch for the Bronze "David"; and Arm Study for the Marble "David"

Pen and ink

THE LOUVRE, PARIS, FRANCE

The Three Crosses

Red chalk

THE BRITISH MUSEUM, LONDON, ENGLAND

Study for Sebastiano del Piombo's Raising of Lazarus
Red chalk
THE BRITISH MUSEUM, LONDON, ENGLAND

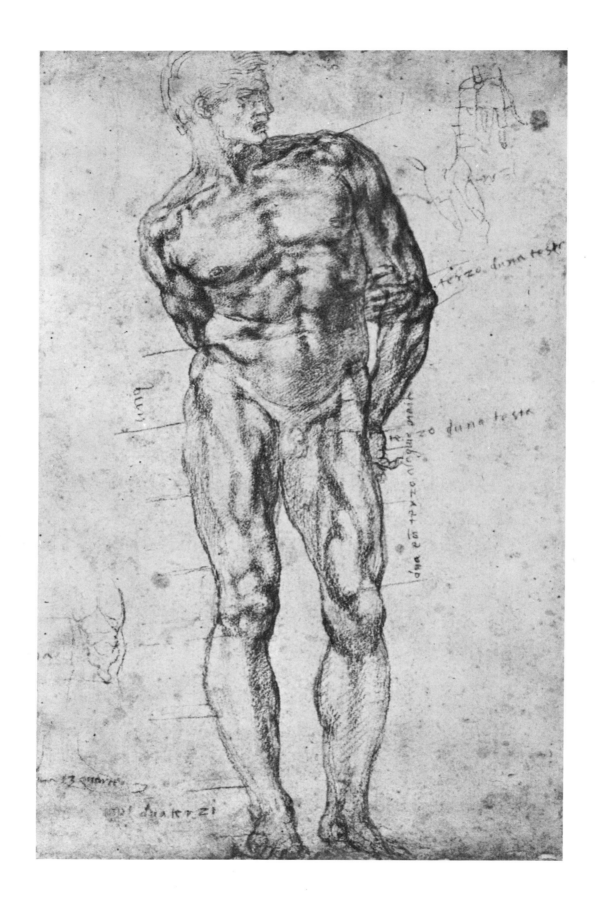

Male Nude with Proportions
Red chalk
WINDSOR CASTLE, ROYAL LIBRARY, BERKSHIRE, ENGLAND

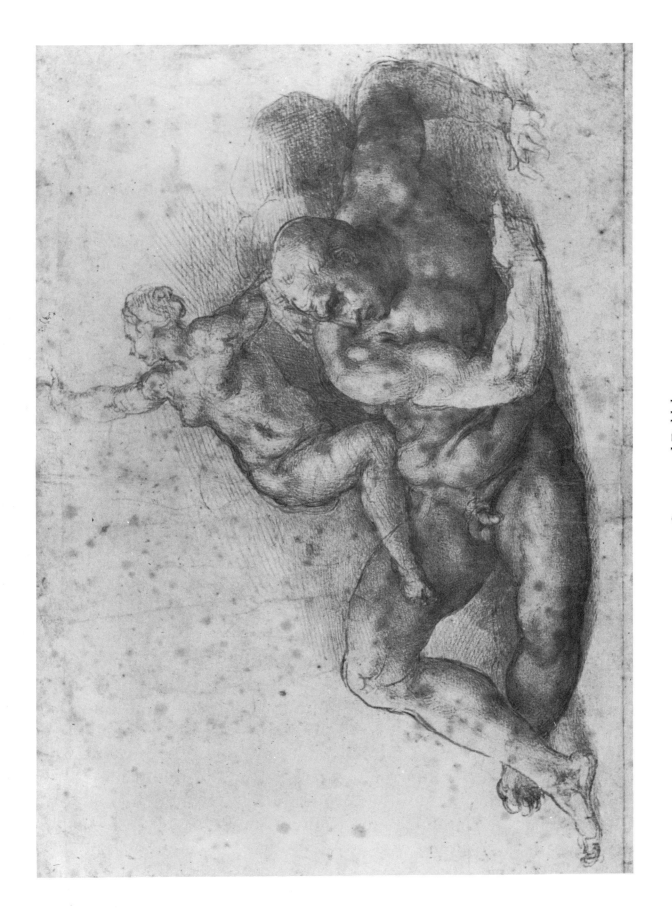

Samson and Delilah

Red chalk

ASHMOLEAN MUSEUM, OXFORD, ENGLAND

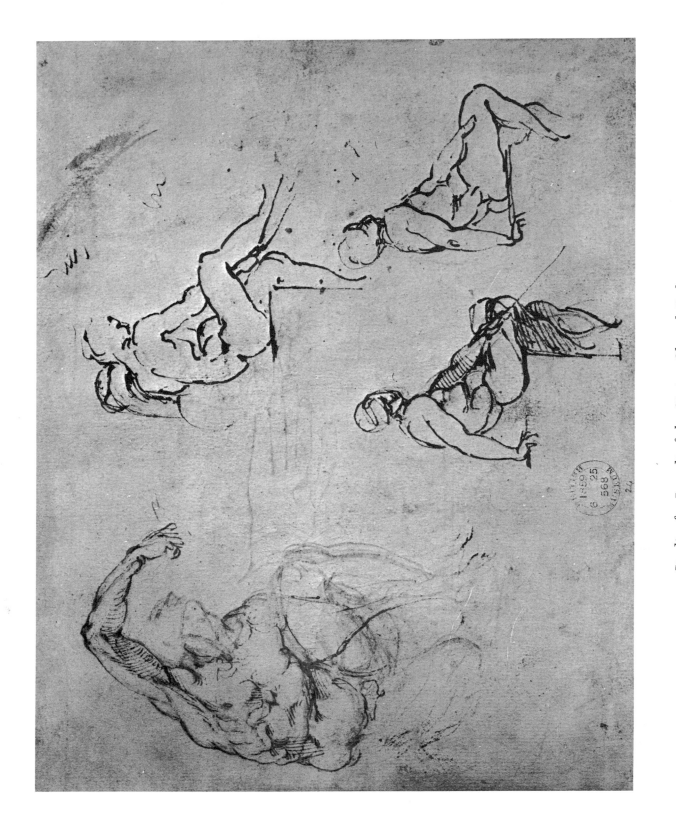

Studies for Ignudi of the Sistine Chapel Ceiling

Black chalk, brown and black ink

THE BRITISH MUSEUM, LONDON, ENGLAND

Damned Soul

Black chalk

UFFIZI GALLERY, FLORENCE, ITALY

Resurrection of Christ
Black chalk
WINDSOR CASTLE, ROYAL LIBRARY, BERKSHIRE, ENGLAND

Saint Anne with the Virgin and Child
Pen and ink and black chalk
THE LOUVRE, PARIS, FRANCE

Head and Figure Study for the "Day of Judgment"
Black chalk

TEYLER MUSEUM, HAARLEM, HOLLAND

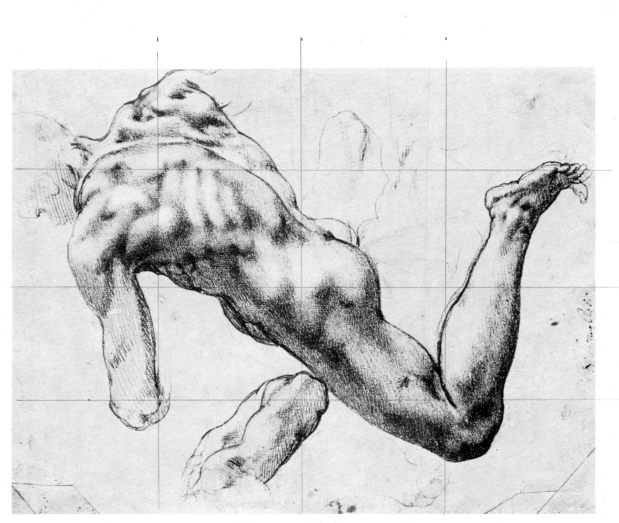

Ignudo
Red chalk

TEYLER MUSEUM, HAARLEM, HOLLAND

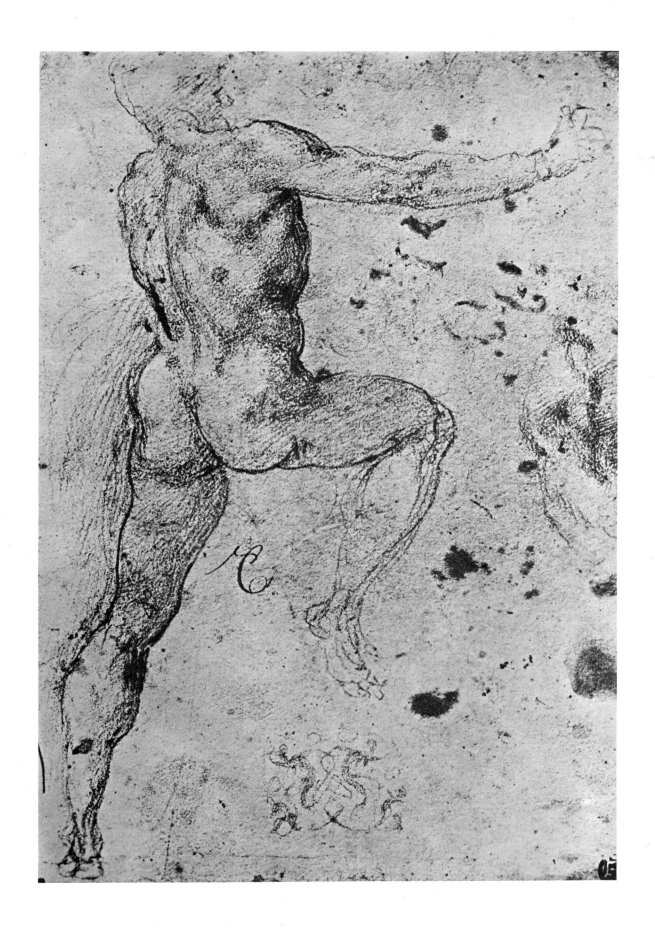

Running Satyr

Black chalk

THE LOUVRE, PARIS, FRANCE

Studies for the "Haman" of the Sistine Frescoes

Red chalk

TEYLER MUSEUM, HAARLEM, HOLLAND

Runner with Lance, Study for the Battle Cartoon

Black chalk

TEYLER MUSEUM, HAARLEM, HOLLAND

The Holy Family

Red chalk

THE DUKE OF PORTLAND, LONDON, ENGLAND

Three Labours of Hercules
Red chalk
WINDSOR CASTLE, ROYAL LIBRARY, BERKSHIRE, ENGLAND

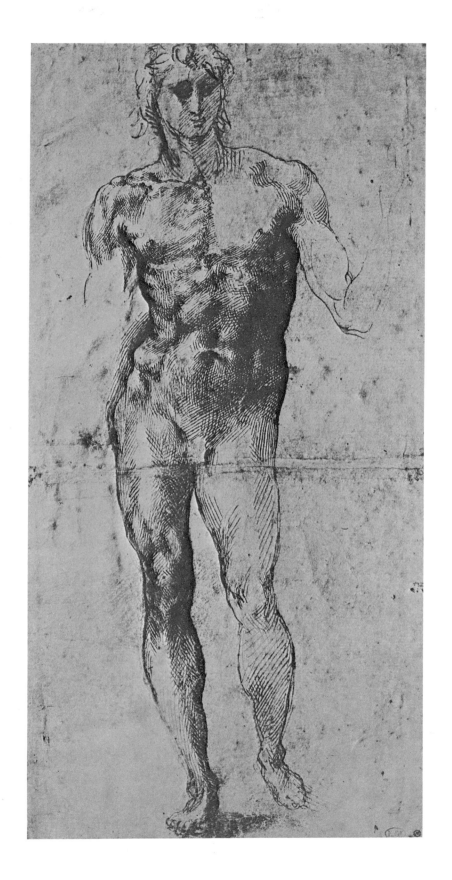

Standing Nude Figure

Pen and ink

THE LOUVRE, PARIS, FRANCE

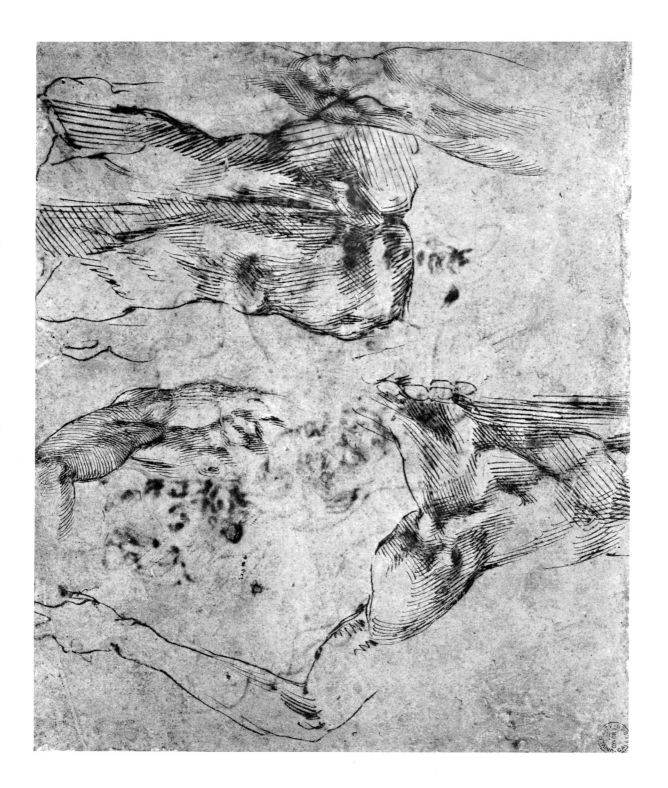

Studies of the Nude
Pen and ink
ASHMOLEAN MUSEUM, OXFORD, ENGLAND

Study for a Figure in the "Resurrection of Christ"

Red chalk

CASA BUONARROTI, FLORENCE, ITALY

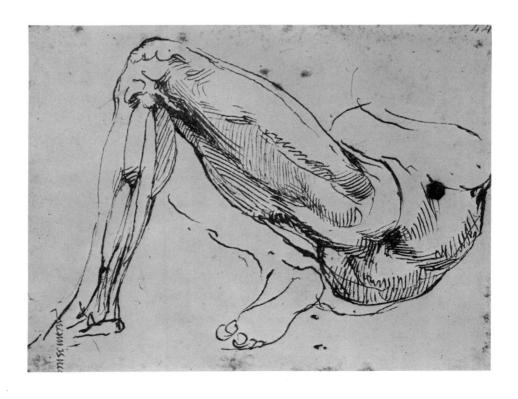

Sketches of Torso and Leg of the "Leda"

Pen and ink

CASA BUONARROTI, FLORENCE, ITALY

Figure Studies for the "Last Judgement"
Black chalk
THE BRITISH MUSEUM, LONDON, ENGLAND

Head Study for the "Leda"
Red chalk
CASA BUONARROTI, FLORENCE, ITALY

Various Figure Studies

Pen and ink

THE LOUVRE, PARIS, FRANCE

Studies for the Libyan Sibyl
Red chalk
COURTESY OF THE METROPOLITAN MUSEUM OF ART, NEW YORK CITY
JOSEPH PULITZER BEQUEST

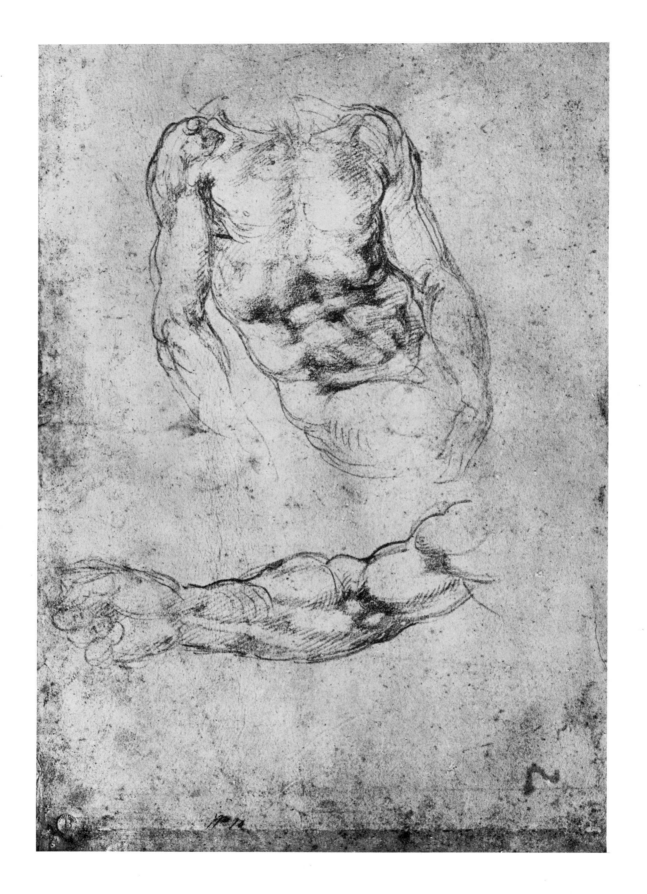

Study for a Pietá
Black chalk
CASA BUONARROTI, FLORENCE, ITALY

The Risen Christ
Black chalk
WINDSOR CASTLE, ROYAL LIBRARY, BERKSHIRE, ENGLAND

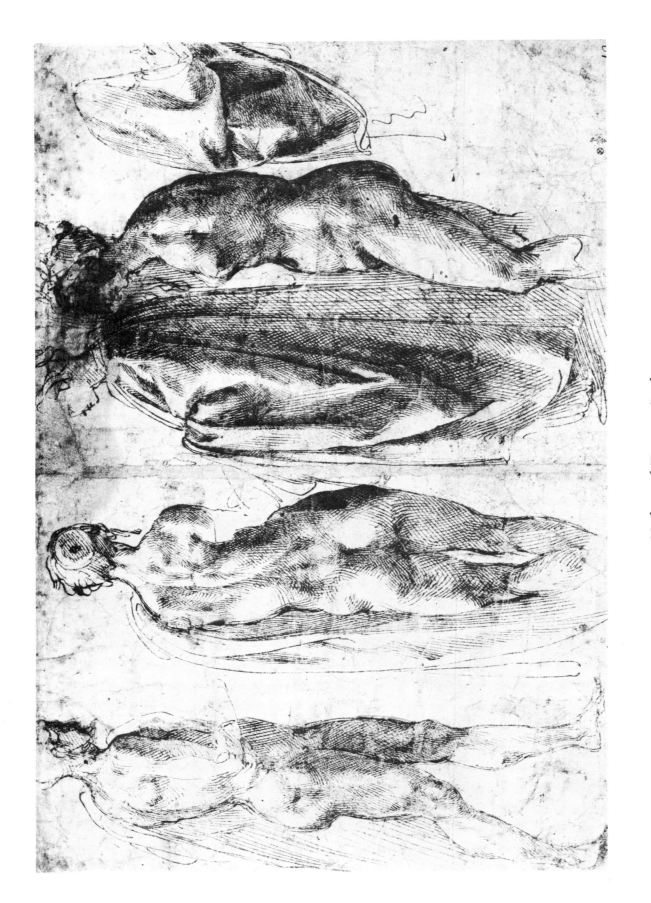

Nudes and Drapery Studies
Pen and ink
MUSEE CONDE, CHANTILLY, FRANCE

First Sketches for the Sistine Ceiling Frescoes
Pen and ink
THE BRITISH MUSEUM, LONDON, ENGLAND

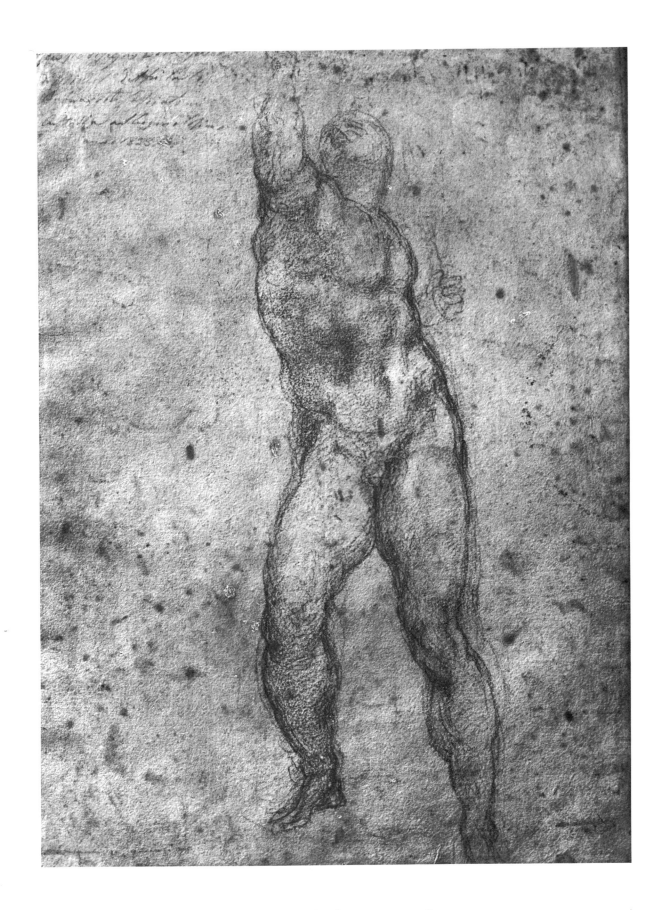

Study for the "Resurrection"
Black chalk
CASA BUONARROTI, FLORENCE, ITALY

A Philosopher
Pen and ink
THE BRITISH MUSEUM, LONDON, ENGLAND

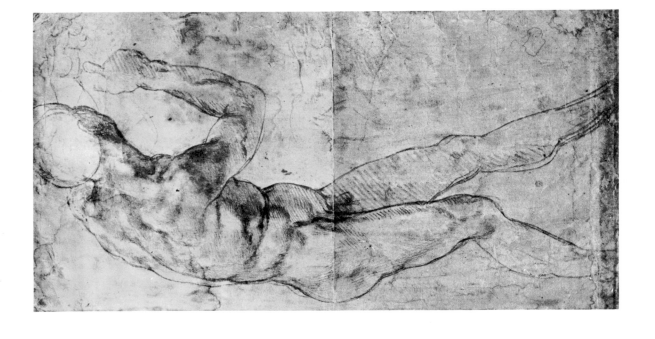

Male Figure Study for the Battle Cartoon
Black chalk
TEYLER MUSEUM, HAARLEM, HOLLAND

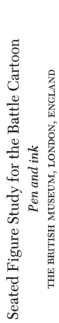

Seated Figure Study for the Battle Cartoon
Pen and ink
THE BRITISH MUSEUM, LONDON, ENGLAND

Virgin and Child with St. John
Black chalk
WINDSOR CASTLE, ROYAL LIBRARY, BERKSHIRE, ENGLAND

Unfinished Study of a Head
Black chalk

WINDSOR CASTLE, ROYAL LIBRARY, BERKSHIRE, ENGLAND

Woman in a Fantastic Dress
Pen and ink
THE BRITISH MUSEUM, LONDON, ENGLAND

Back View of Male Figure, After an Antique Relief
Pen and ink
CASA BUONARROTI, FLORENCE, ITALY

Head Study

Black chalk

THE LOUVRE, PARIS, FRANCE

Male Torso
Black chalk
BRITISH MUSEUM, LONDON, ENGLAND

Study for the Head of Zechariah of the Sistine Frescoes
Black chalk
UFFIZI GALLERY, FLORENCE, ITALY

Studies of a Reclining Male Nude

Red chalk

THE BRITISH MUSEUM, LONDON, ENGLAND

Archers Shooting at a Herm
Red chalk

WINDSOR CASTLE, ROYAL LIBRARY, BERKSHIRE, ENGLAND

Girl Holding a Distaff
Black chalk
BRITISH MUSEUM, LONDON, ENGLAND

Studies for the Medici Madonna

Pen and ink

THE LOUVRE, PARIS, FRANCE

Study for a Pietá
Black chalk
THE LOUVRE, PARIS, FRANCE